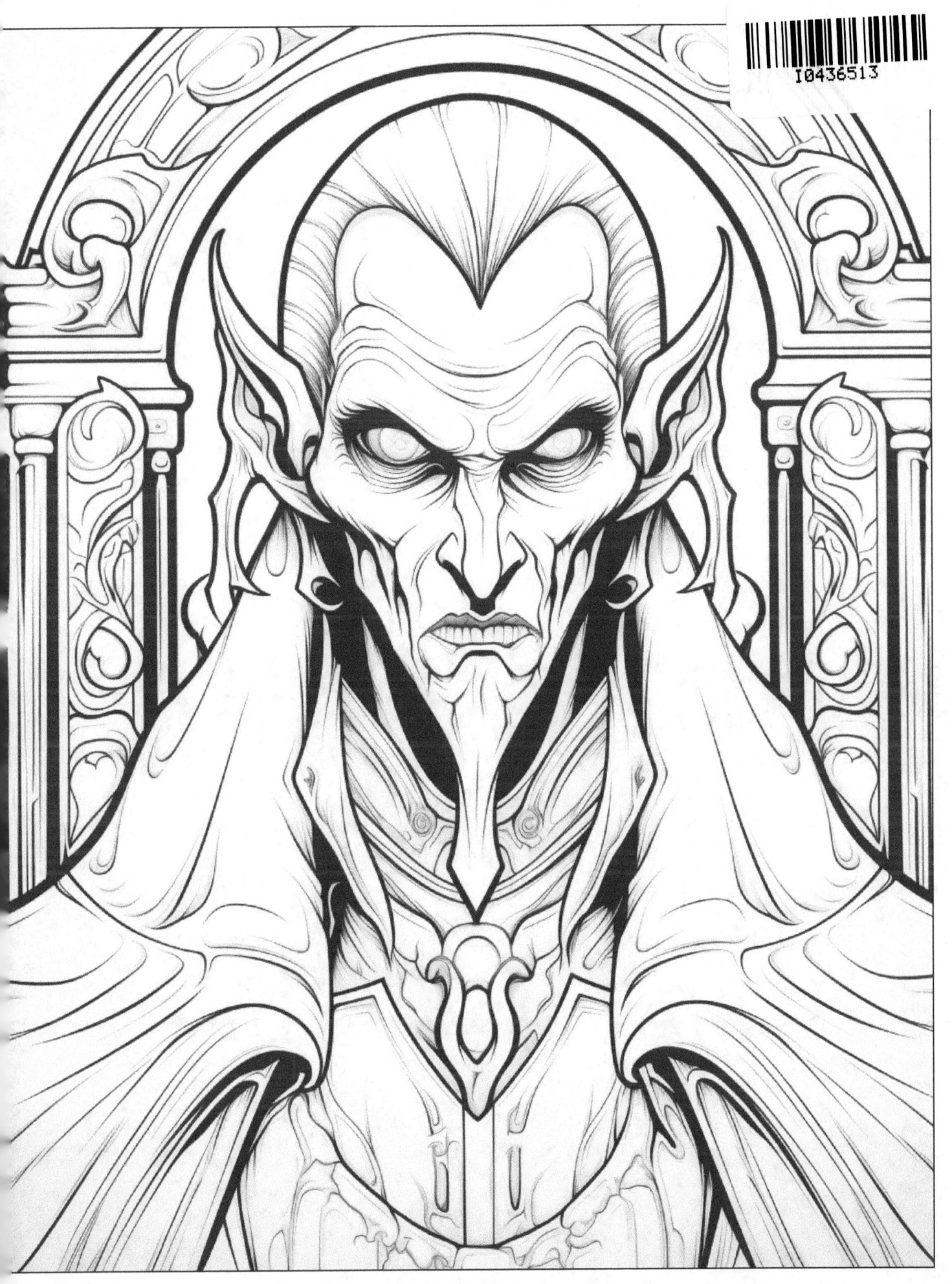

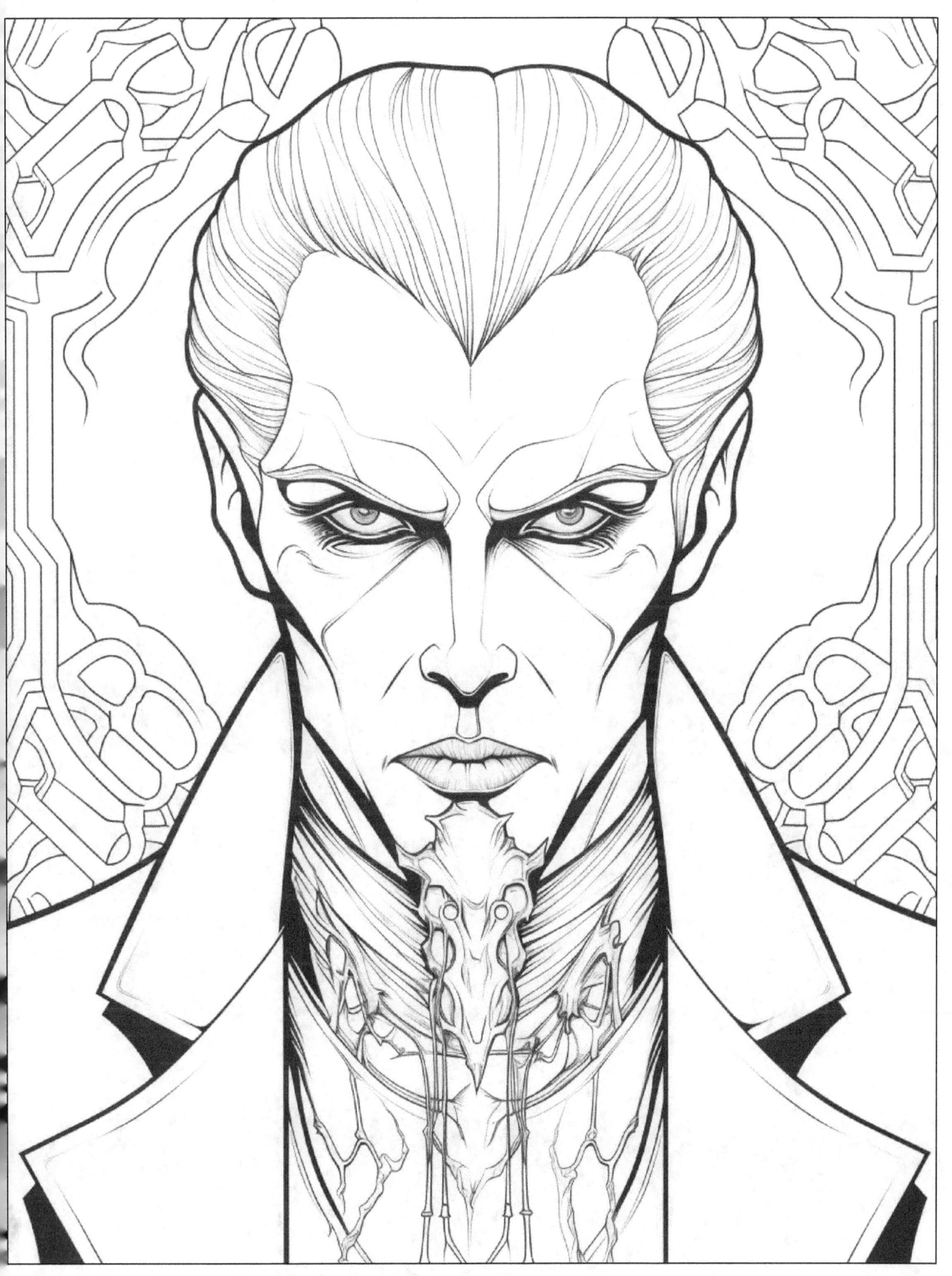

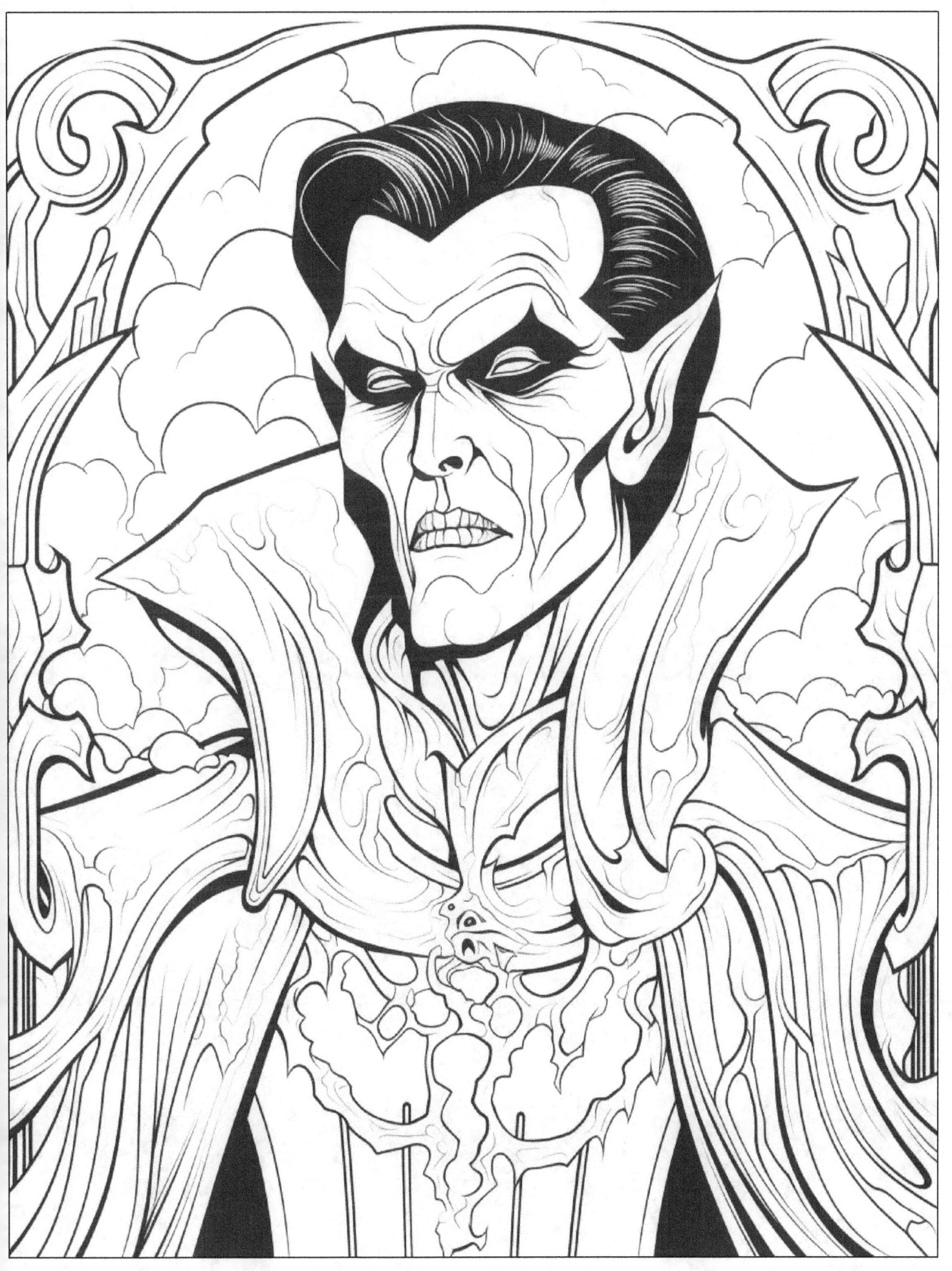

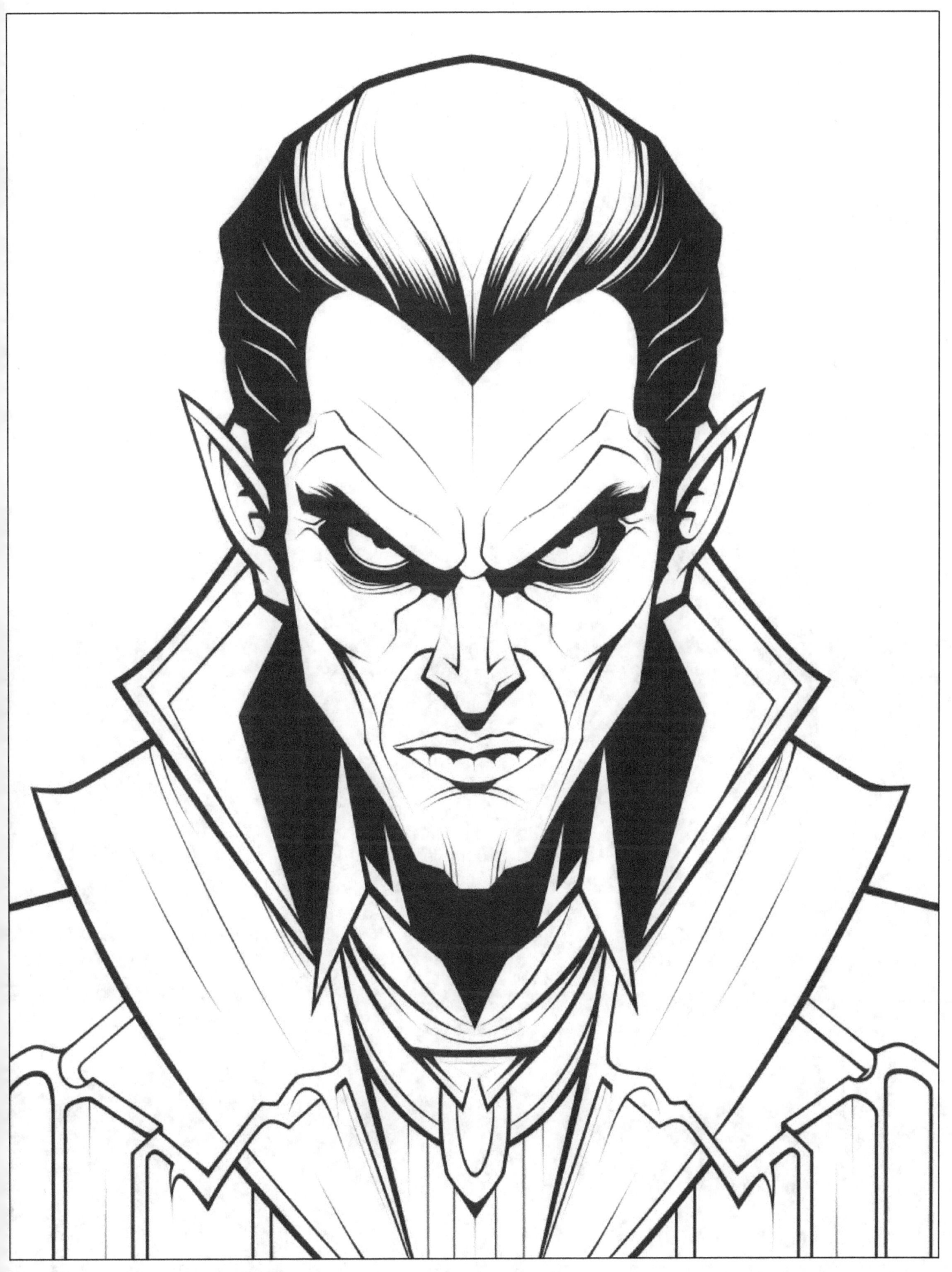

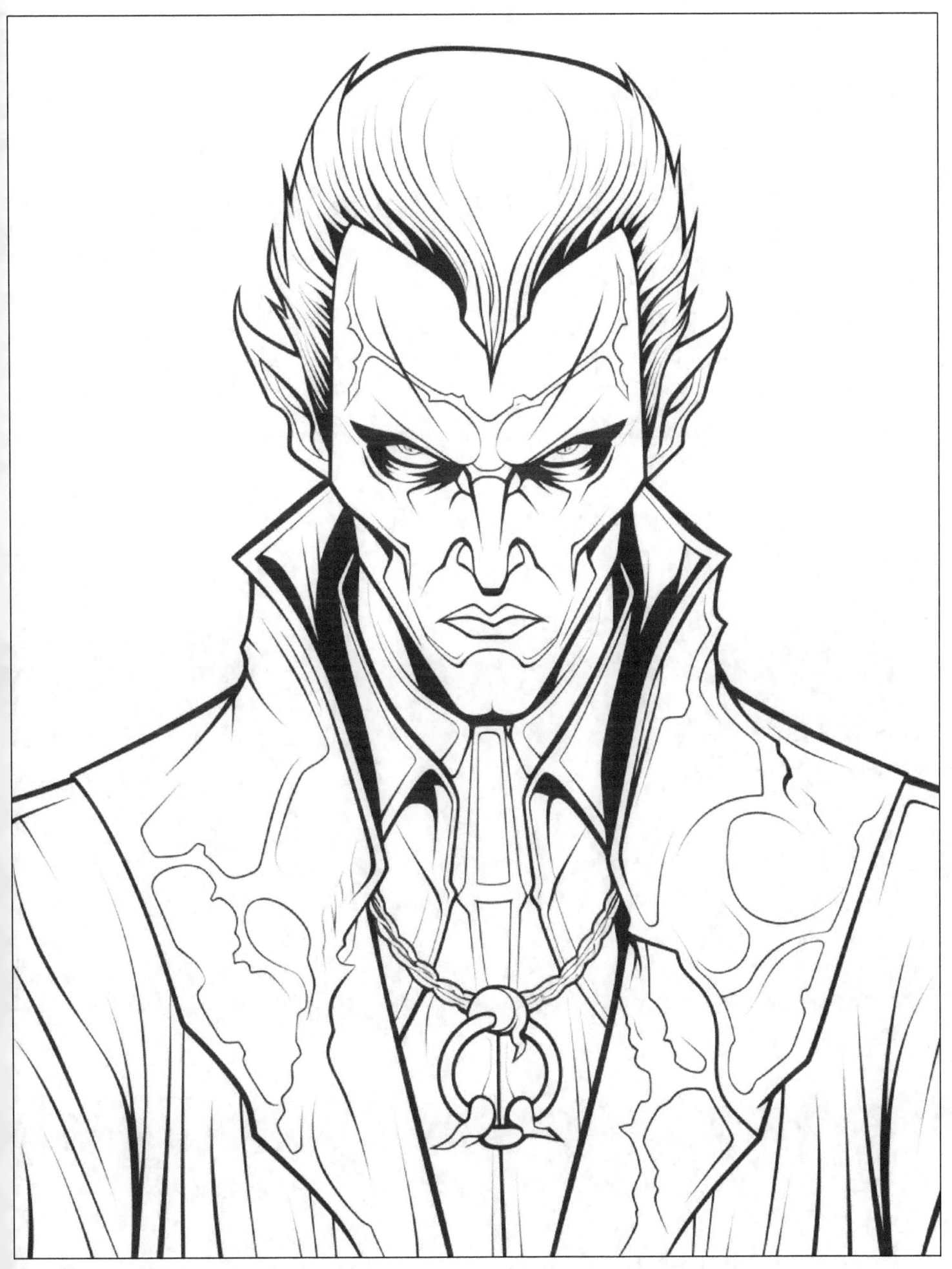

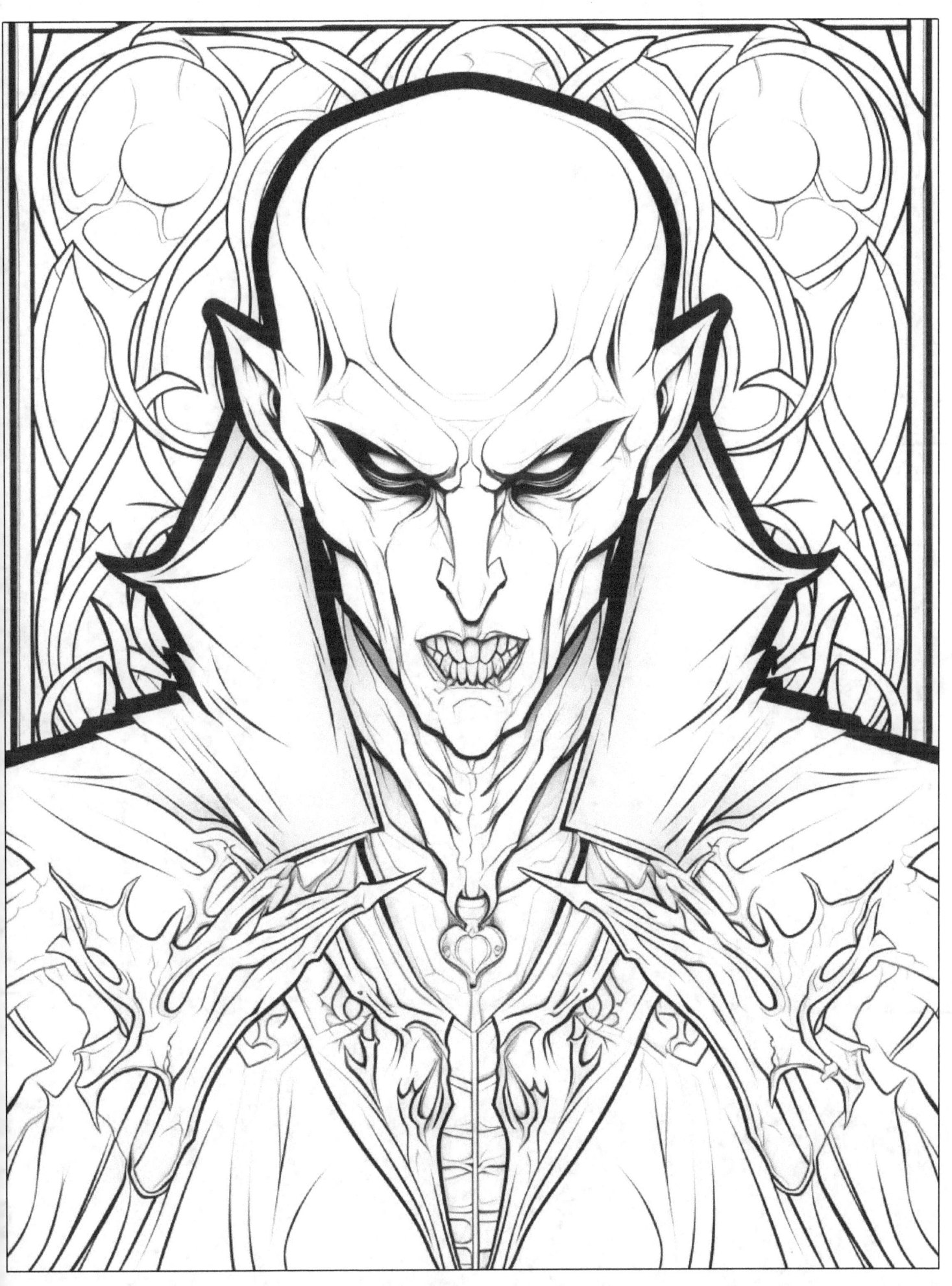

ColorQuest Collections

Fun and creative coloring books for all ages

For more fun and creative coloring books, search for ColorQuest Collections in your favorite bookstore!

www.ingramcontent.com/pod-product-compliance
Lightning Source LLC
Chambersburg PA
CBHW080837310526
45796CB00015B/307